Football By the Numbers

Mary Elizabeth Salzmann

Consulting Editor, Diane Craig, M.A./Reading Specialist

Published by ABDO Publishing Company, 8000 West 78th Street, Edina, Minnesota 55439.

Printed in the United States.

Editor: Katherine Hengel
Content Developer: Nancy Tuminelly
Cover and Interior Design and Production: Colleen Dolphin, Mighty Media
Photo Credits: Brand X Pictures, iStockphoto (Gene Chutka), Photodisc, Shutterstock

Library of Congress Cataloging-in-Publication Data

Library of Congress Cataloging-in-Publication Data

Salzmann, Mary Elizabeth, 1968-
Football by the numbers / Mary Elizabeth Salzmann.
p. cm. -- (Team sports by the numbers)
ISBN 978-1-60453-769-7
1. Football--Juvenile literature. 2. Arithmetic--Juvenile literature. I. Title.
GV950.7.S25 2010
796.332--dc22

2009029861

SandCastle™ Level: Fluent

SandCastle™ books are created by a team of professional educators, reading specialists, and content developers around five essential components—phonemic awareness, phonics, vocabulary, text comprehension, and fluency—to assist young readers as they develop reading skills and strategies and increase their general knowledge. All books are written, reviewed, and leveled for guided reading, early reading intervention, and Accelerated Reader® programs for use in shared, guided, and independent reading and writing activities to support a balanced approach to literacy instruction. The SandCastle™ series has four levels that correspond to early literacy development. The levels are provided to help teachers and parents select appropriate books for young readers.

Emerging Readers
(no flags)

Beginning Readers
(1 flag)

Transitional Readers
(2 flags)

Fluent Readers
(3 flags)

SandCastle™ would like to hear from you. Please send us your comments and suggestions.
sandcastle@abdopublishing.com

Contents

Introduction.......... 4

The Football Field.......... 5

The Game.......... 6

Offense.......... 9

Defense.......... 17

Football Facts.......... 22

Answers to By the Numbers!.......... 23

Glossary.......... 24

Introduction

Numbers are used all the time in football.

- A touchdown is 6 points.
- A football is about 11 inches (28 cm) long.
- An overtime period lasts 15 minutes.
- It is 30 feet (9.1 m) from the ground to the top of the goalposts.
- A field goal is 3 points.
- The lines that go across the field are 5 yards (4.6 m) **apart**.

Let's learn more about how numbers are used in football.

The Football Field

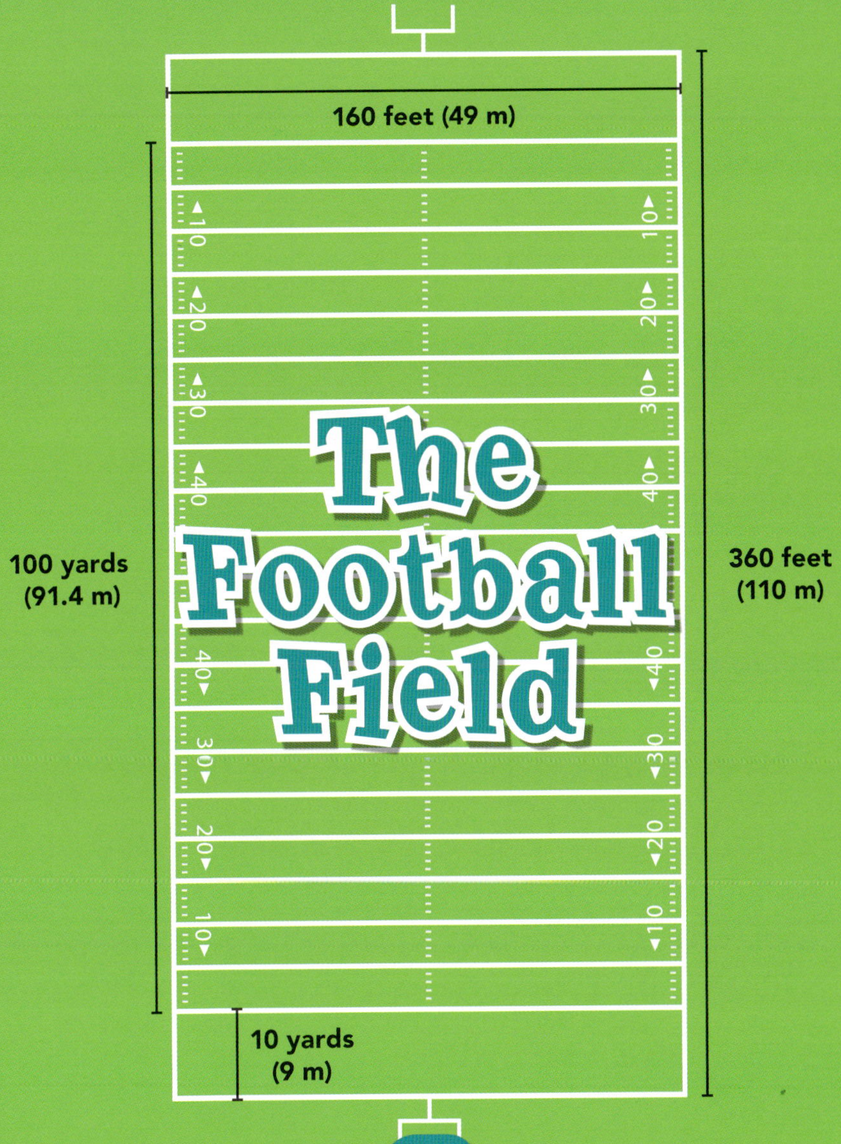

160 feet (49 m)

100 yards (91.4 m)

360 feet (110 m)

10 yards (9 m)

10 20 30 40 40 30 20 10

The Game

In football, the game time is 60 minutes. During a game, 11 players from each team play at a time.

Each team tries to get the ball into the other team's end zone. One team has 4 tries to move the ball at least 10 yards (3 m). If they make it, they get a first down. If they don't make it, it's the other team's turn.

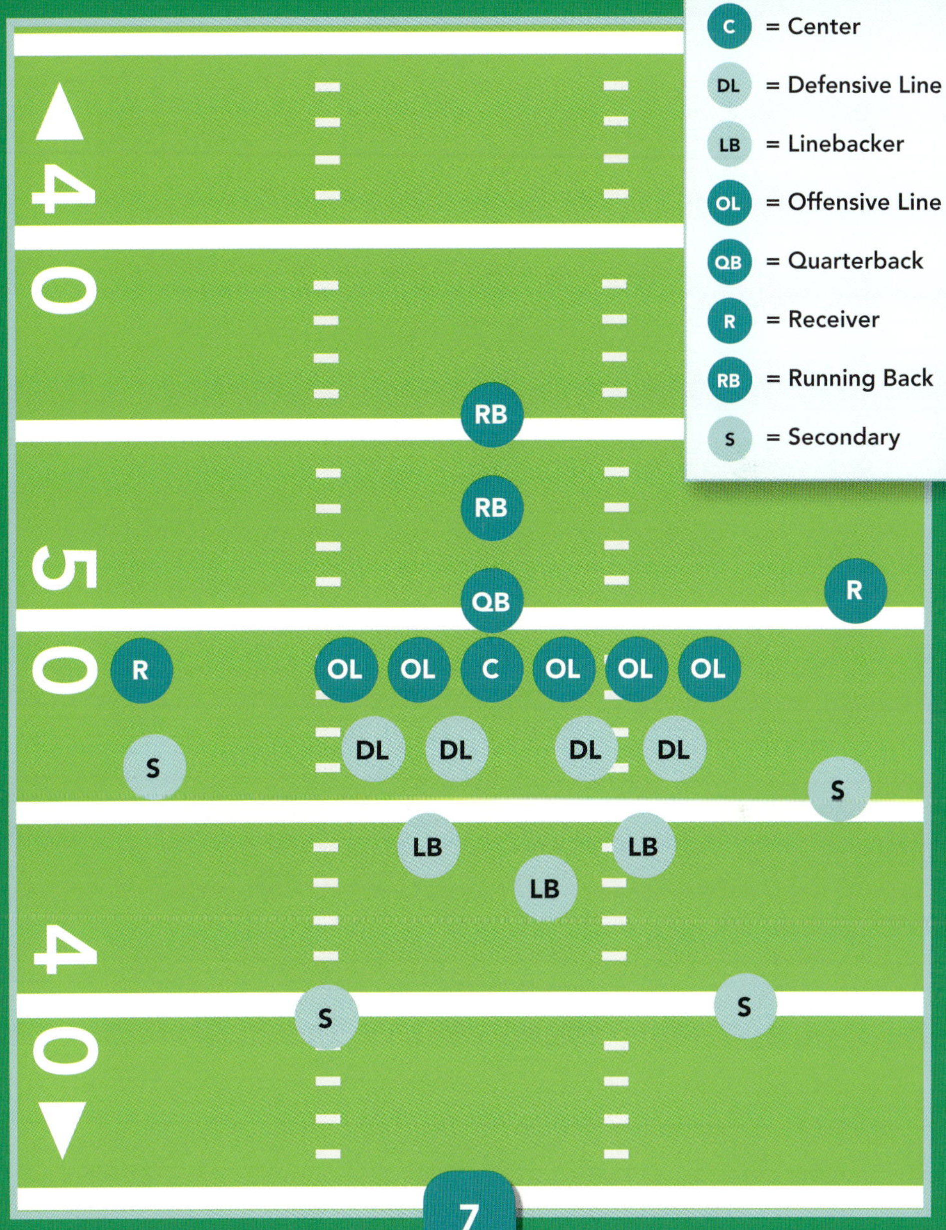
C = Center
DL = Defensive Line
LB = Linebacker
OL = Offensive Line
QB = Quarterback
R = Receiver
RB = Running Back
S = Secondary
40
50
40
RB
RB
QB
R
R
OL
OL
C
OL
OL
OL
S
DL
DL
DL
DL
S
LB
LB
LB
S
S

50

Offense

The team trying to score is the offense.

Austin is the quarterback. He gets ready to throw a pass.

By the Numbers!

A

Austin passed the ball 9 times. He had 5 **completions**. How many times were his passes incomplete?

(answer on p. 23)

David is a receiver. He catches a pass from the quarterback.

By the Numbers!

B

David caught 2 passes in the first half. He caught 3 passes in the second half. How many passes did David catch in the game?

(answer on p. 23)

Josh is a running back. He tries to carry the ball far enough for a first down.

By the Numbers!

C

Josh's team needs to move the ball 10 yards for a first down. Josh carried it 4 yards. How many more yards does his team need to get a first down?

(answer on p. 23)

Eli is a placekicker. After his team scores a touchdown, he kicks the extra point.

By the Numbers!

D Eli's team scores a touchdown for 6 points. If Eli's kick goes between the goalposts, they will get 1 more point. How many points will they have?

(answer on p. 23)

Defense

The team trying to keep the other team from scoring is the defense.

Matt is a linebacker. After the **snap**, he will try to **sack** the other team's quarterback.

By the Numbers!

E Matt sacked the quarterback 2 times. His teammate Dylan also sacked the quarterback 2 times. Together, how many times did they sack the quarterback?

(answer on p. 23)

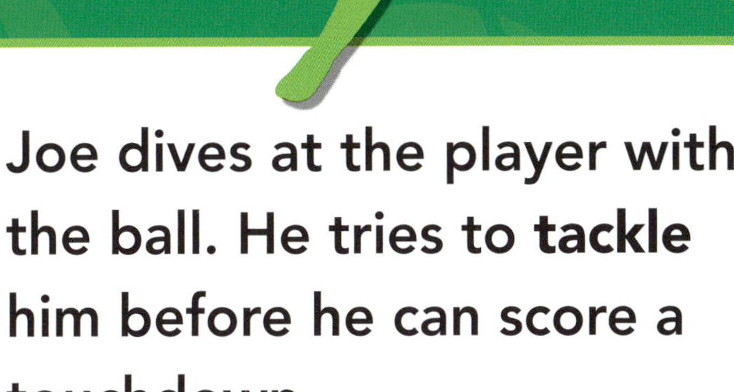

Joe dives at the player with the ball. He tries to **tackle** him before he can score a touchdown.

By the Numbers!

F

Joe's team has 7 touchdowns. The other team has 4 touchdowns. How many more touchdowns does Joe's team have?

(answer on p. 23)

18
17

Ethan is a defensive lineman. He will try to stop the other team's receiver from catching a pass.

By the Numbers!

G

The other team has 4 tries to get a first down. This is their second try. If Ethan's team stops them on this play, how many more tries will they have?

(answer on p. 23)

Football Facts

- Jerry Rice caught 1,549 passes for a total of 22,895 yards in his **career**. He scored 197 touchdowns.
- From 1957 to 1969, the Cleveland Browns scored at least one touchdown per game 166 games in a row.
- In his career, Emmitt Smith **rushed** for 18,355 yards. He scored 164 touchdowns.
- No NFL player is allowed to wear the numbers 0 or 00 on his jersey.
- Morten Andersen played in 382 games in 25 NFL seasons.
- Kickers Tom Dempsey and Jason Elam both made 63-yard field goals.

Answers to By the Numbers!

A

$$\begin{array}{r} 9 \\ -5 \\ \hline 4 \end{array}$$

Austin passed the ball 9 times. He had 5 **completions**. How many times were his passes **incomplete**?

B

$$\begin{array}{r} 2 \\ +3 \\ \hline 5 \end{array}$$

David caught 2 passes in the first half. He caught 3 passes in the second half. How many passes did David catch in the game?

C

$$\begin{array}{r} 10 \\ -4 \\ \hline 6 \end{array}$$

Josh's team needs to move the ball 10 yards for a first down. Josh carried it 4 yards. How many more yards does his team need to get a first down?

D

$$\begin{array}{r} 6 \\ +1 \\ \hline 7 \end{array}$$

Eli's team scores a touchdown for six points. If Eli's kick goes between the goalposts, they will get 1 more point. How many points will they have?

E

$$\begin{array}{r} 2 \\ +2 \\ \hline 4 \end{array}$$

Matt **sacked** the quarterback 2 times. His teammate Dylan also sacked the quarterback 2 times. Together, how many times did they sack the quarterback?

F

$$\begin{array}{r} 7 \\ -4 \\ \hline 3 \end{array}$$

Joe's team has 7 touchdowns. The other team has 4 touchdowns. How many more touchdowns does Joe's team have?

G

$$\begin{array}{r} 4 \\ -2 \\ \hline 2 \end{array}$$

The other team has 4 tries to get a first down. This is their second try. If Ethan's team stops them on this play, how many more tries will they have?

Glossary

apart – away from each other.

career – the work or jobs done over a period of time.

completion – a pass that is caught by a receiver.

incomplete – not caught by an offensive player.

rush – to move the football with a running play rather than a passing play.

sack – to stop a quarterback when he still has the ball and hasn't gained any yards.

snap – when the center passes the football to the quarterback.

tackle – to knock another player down.

To see a complete list of SandCastle™ books and other nonfiction titles from ABDO Publishing Company, visit www.abdopublishing.com.
8000 West 78th Street, Edina, MN 55439 • 800-800-1312 • fax 952-831-1632